# What is Soul In Focus?

Soul In Focus is an inspirational ministry combining photographs of the beauty and wonder of God's creation and the Words of Scripture, along with our thoughts and prayers, to honor God and remind us of how much God loves us and cares for and about us.

# Who is Soul In Focus?

Soul In Focus is Andre Watkins, a 3rd generation photography enthusiast and graduate of New York Institute of Photography, Lori Watkins, an inspirational writer and creator of Fearless Bible Investigators, and our daughters Cheri Sepasi and Kharmen Watkins who provide support.

Oh, that men would give thanks to the Lord for His goodness, and for His wonderful works to the children of men!
For He satisfies the longing soul, and fills the hungry soul with goodness.
Psalm 107:8-9

YO-EKP-415

"Call to Me, and I will answer you, and show you great and mighty things, which you do not know."
Jeremiah 33:3

I STOOD UP TO GOD AND CRIED OUT,
"WHEN WILL YOU HANDLE MY SITUATION?!"
HE POINTED TO A FLOWER AND REPLIED,
"TELL ME HOW, FROM A SEED, DID I CREATE THIS DESIGN TO UNFOLD?"
I BOWED DOWN BEFORE GOD,TOOK BACK MY SITUATION, AND GAVE HIM MY LIFE.

YOU WERE CREATED TO BE REGAL,
A PLACE OF  PROTECTION, A SANCTUARY HOVERING
WHERE WEARY SOULS CAN  QUIETLY BREATHE,
AND FIND LIFE BENEATH YOUR COVERING

"He who dwells
in the secret
place of the
Most High shall
abide under the
shadow of the
Almighty."
Psalm 91:1

"The Lord has
appeared of old
to me, saying:
'Yes, I have loved
you with an
everlasting love;
Therefore with
loving kindness
I have drawn
you.'"
Jeremiah 31:3

GOD'S WHISPER IS A GENTLE BREEZE HIS SMILE A WARM EMBRACE
HIS LOVE A ROLLING SEA WASHING OVER US WITH GRACE
TODAY MAY YOU HEAR GOD'S WHISPER, FEEL HIS SMILE
AND BE OVERWHELMED BY HIS LOVE

I AM A WORK OF ART, SCULPTED
AND PAINTED WITH BRILLIANT
HUES; BUT BY UNSEEN HANDS

I AM FORMED WITH SYMMETRY,
METICULOUSLY DESIGNED WITH
NO PATTERN OR PLAN

I AM SEPARATE PIECES, INTRICATELY
CUT AND JOINED TOGETHER BY
NO MACHINERY OF MAN

I AM A MIRACLE, A TESTIMONY,
I REPRESENT THE GOD WHO CAN!

"Behold, I am
the Lord, the
God of all flesh.
Is there anything
too hard for
Me?"
Jeremiah 32:27

NOTHING AROUND ME CAN I PERCEIVE,
HEAVY IS THE AIR I BREATHE,

SPEECH IS MUFFLED, IMAGES BLURRED,
WORDS STRUGGLE TO BE HEARD

HEART IS HEAVY, THOUGHTS ARE MIRED,
WITH EVERY BREATH I BREATHE I TIRE,

YET EVEN IN THIS STATE I'M IN,
YOU DO NOT FORCE ME TO PRETEND

YOU WALK BESIDE ME, TO YOU I CLEAVE,
TOGETHER THIS HEAVY AIR WE BREATHE

"Yea, though
I walk through
the valley of the
shadow of death,
I will fear no evil;
for You are
with me…"
Psalm 23:4

WHEN I FEEL BLUE, I FLUTTER MY WINGS AND
REFLECT ON JUST HOW FAR YOU'VE BROUGHT ME

"...being confident of this very thing, that He who has begun a good work in you will complete it until the day of Jesus Christ."
Philippians 1:6

YOU SEE MY MIXED-UP WORLD AND YOU STEP INTO IT AND SEPARATE ME FROM MY DARKNESS AND THERE IS LIGHT

YOU WHISPER TO THE CLOUDS AND THEY MOVE AND THE OCEANS DRAW UP AND REVEAL LAND
LAND, SEA, AND SKY ARE TEEMING WITH LIFE YOU CREATED A WHOLE NEW WORLD FOR ME NOW MY MIND IS AT REST AND IT IS GOOD

"Create in me a clean heart, O God, and renew a steadfast spirit within me."
Psalm 51:10

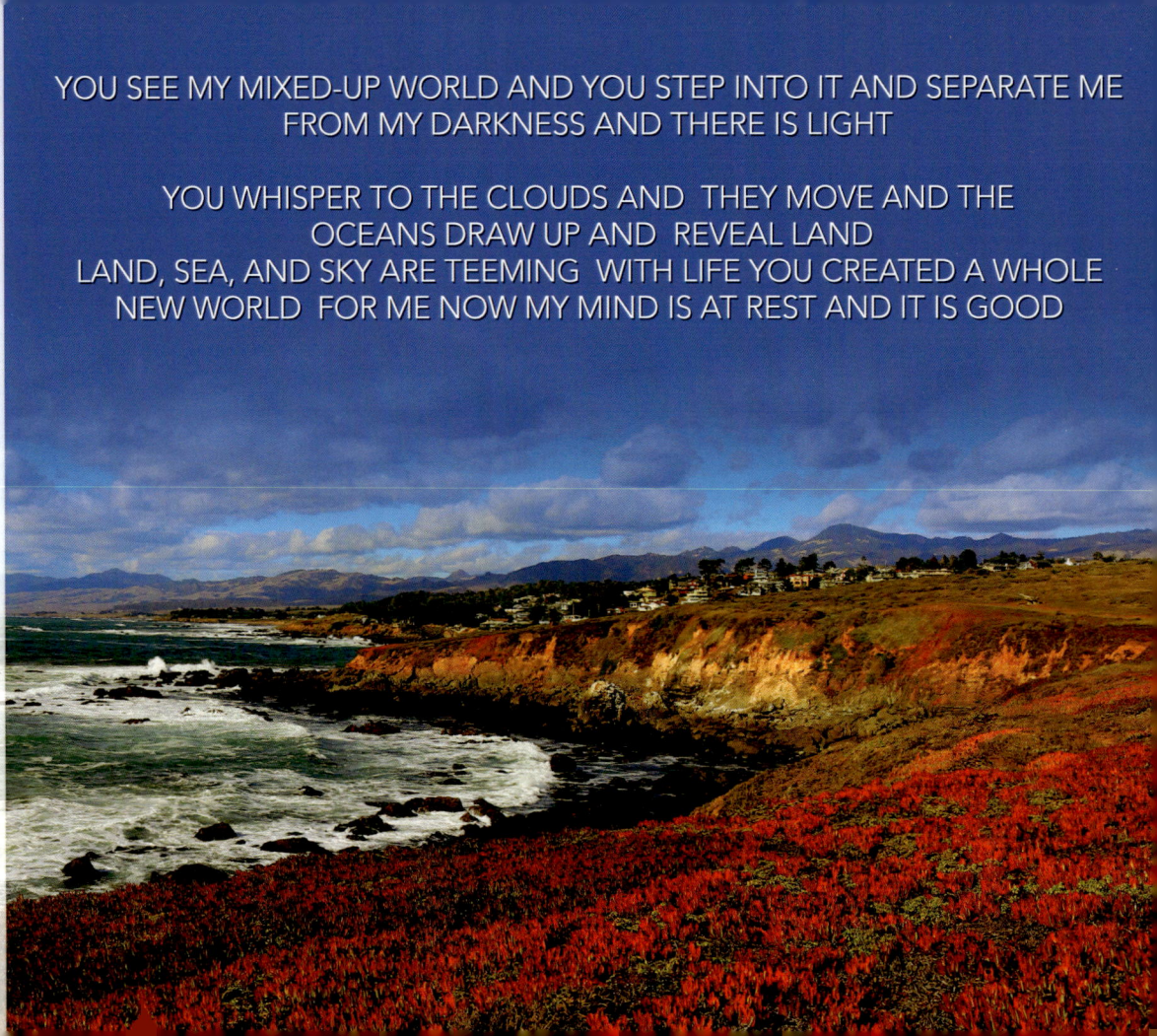

MAY THE PEACE OF GOD CALM YOUR SOUL
WHISPER SOFTLY TO YOUR SPIRIT
AND GENTLY TOUCH YOUR HEART

"You will keep him in perfect peace, whose mind is stayed on You, because he trusts in You."
Isaiah 26:3

"For You have been a strength to the poor, a strength to the needy in his distress, a refuge from the storm, a shade from the heat…"
Isaiah 25:4

THE TREES BOW BEFORE YOU AND CREATE A CANOPY,
WAITING FOR LIFE'S WOUNDED IN HUMBLE EXPECTANCY
FOR THE HURTING AND THE WEARY, THE FAINT-HEARTED AND THE ILL,
TO BE A COVER FOR THEIR JOURNEY AND A QUIET PLACE TO HEAL

MAY EVERY RAINDROP FROM THE SKY
REMIND YOU THAT FOR YOU HE CRIES,
FOR YOUR SORROW, FOR YOUR PAIN
FOR YOU TO SEE YOUR LOVED ONE AGAIN,
FOR WHEN YOU HURT, HE HURTS TOO
AND EVERY TEAR HE SHEDS FOR YOU

"You number my
wanderings;
Put my tears into
Your bottle;
Are they not in
Your book?"
Isaiah 56:8

"He will bless
those who fear
the Lord, both
small and great."
Psalm 115:13

I MAY BE SMALL, BUT
YOU TOOK JUST AS MUCH
CARE IN MAKING ME AS
BEAUTIFUL AS ANY  CREATURE

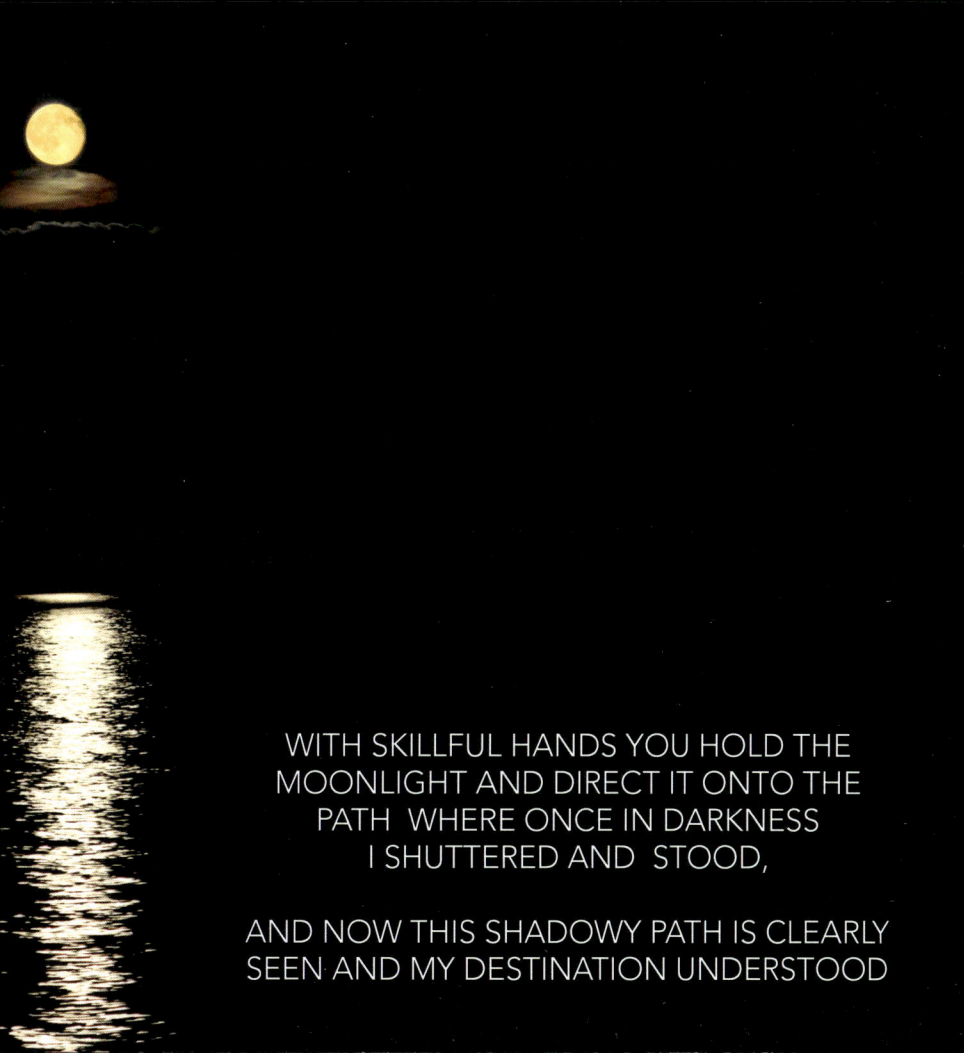

WITH SKILLFUL HANDS YOU HOLD THE
MOONLIGHT AND DIRECT IT ONTO THE
PATH  WHERE ONCE IN DARKNESS
I SHUTTERED AND  STOOD,

AND NOW THIS SHADOWY PATH IS CLEARLY
SEEN AND MY DESTINATION UNDERSTOOD

"Trust in the
Lord with all your
heart, and lean
not on your own
understanding;
In all your ways
acknowledge
Him, and He
shall direct your
paths."
Proverbs 3:5-6

"He shall cover you with His feathers, and under His wings you shall take refuge;His truth shall be *your* shield and buckler."
Psalm 91:4

I CAN CLAIM YOUR PROMISES BECAUSE YOU CLAIMED...ME

WHEN I THOUGHT THAT I WAS
LEFT TO BE ALONE
I TURNED AND SAW THAT YOU
WERE ALWAYS THERE WITH ME

"And the Lord,
He is the One
who goes before
you.  He will be
with you, He will
not
leave you nor
forsake you;
do not fear nor
be dismayed."
Deuteronomy
31:8

OPEN YOURSELF UP TO GOD
AND EXPERIENCE:

NEW LIFE –
HE WANTS FOR YOU

NEW POSSIBILITIES –
HE HAS FOR YOU

NEW JOYS –
HE GIVES TO YOU

"Therefore, if anyone is in Christ, he is a new creation; old things have passed away; behold, all things have become new."
2 Corinthians 5:17

DURING THE CLOUDIEST TIMES IN LIFE, I STILL FEEL AND SEE YOUR PRESENCE

"Arise, shine; for your light has come! And the glory of the Lord is risen upon you."
Isaiah 60:1

THANK YOU, LORD, FOR WHEN CONSIDERING ALL THE POSSIBLE SOLUTIONS TO MY PROBLEMS, YOU NEVER CHOSE REJECTING ME AS AN OPTION

"You open Your hand and satisfy the desire of every living thing."
Psalm 145:16

YOUR WAY IS NOT ALWAYS
DIRECT BUT IT ALWAYS
ENDS UP AT YOUR
DETERMINED PLACE

"I will go
before you
and make the
crooked places
straight…"
Isaiah 45:2

IF I CAN TRULY DO ALL
THINGS THROUGH CHRIST
WHO STRENGTHENS ME,
THE FIRST THING I WILL DO
IS PLACE ALL MY TRUST IN
HIM TO CARE FOR ME

"Oh, taste and
see that the Lord
is good; Blessed
is the man who
trusts in Him!"
Psalm 34:8

WHEN YOU CAN'T DISCERN
*GOD SEES*

WHEN YOU CAN'T ADVANCE
*GOD MOVES*

WHEN YOU CAN'T MANAGE
*GOD LEADS*

"To give light to those who sit in darkness and the shadow of death, To guide our feet into the way of peace."
Luke 1:79

"These all wait for You, that You may give them their food in due season."
Psalm 104:27

GOD GATHERS THE SEA ONTO THE SHORE
FOR CHOICE INGREDIENTS FROM THE OCEAN'S FLOOR
NOW DAWN IS LIT ON THE WAVERING SEAS
AND SALTY AIR CARRIED BY OCEAN BREEZE
WE AWAKEN TO CAWING SEA GULL SOUNDS
AND A BUFFET SET FOR MILES AROUND
THE SHORE IS TRIMMED IN WHITE FOAM LACE
AND WITH GRATEFUL HEARTS WE BOW FOR GRACE

WHEN STORM CLOUDS GATHER AND
WORRIES SWIRL ROUND
I TAKE REFUGE AMONG THE HILLS AND
BOLT FAITH TO THE GROUND
I COVER MYSELF IN GOD'S PROMISES
AND PRAY TO BE AT PEACE
SWIFTLY YOU STAND UP TO MY STORM
AND COMMAND FOR IT TO CEASE

"…they cry out
to the Lord in
their trouble,
and He brings
them out of their
distresses.
He calms the
storm, so that its
waves are still."
Psalm 107:28-29

"What then shall we say to these things? If God is for us, who can be against us?"
Romans 8:31

SOMETIMES I JUST WANT TO BURY MYSELF IN MY SADNESS, MY HURT, MY SHAME OR MY SORROWS, BUT YOU REMIND ME THAT YOU COVER MY ISSUES, AND ME, IN YOUR GRACE

THE BLESSING THAT I SEE IS ONLY A SMALL PART
OF THE BLESSING YOU HAVE PLANNED FOR ME

"I will give you
the treasures of
darkness and
hidden riches of
secret places,
that you may
know
that I, the Lord…
call you by your
name…"
Isaiah 45:3

"For our light affliction, which is but for a moment, is working for us a far more exceeding and eternal weight of glory," 2 Corinthians 4:17

NOT EVERYTHING THAT LANDS ON US IS MEANT TO STAY WITH US

I LIVED UNDER THE SHADOW OF DARKNESS
WEIGHED DOWN BY CIRCUMSTANCES,
RESTRICTED BY MY SITUATION
UNTIL I PUSHED THROUGH MY LIMITATIONS
TO RISE UP TO GOD'S EXPECTATIONS

"But you are
a chosen
generation, a
royal priesthood,
a holy nation,
His own special
people, that
You may
proclaim the
praises of Him
who called
you out of
darkness into His
marvelous light;"
1 Peter 2:9

AS I TRAVEL ON THIS WINDY BARREN ROAD,
I RELY ON MAN-MADE DEVICES AND FOLLOW AS I'M TOLD
BUT FOR LIFE'S TWISTS AND TURNS I WILL TRUST THE GOD WHO
CREATED ME BECAUSE HE KNOWS JUST
WHERE I AM AND WHERE I NEED TO BE

"Cause me to hear Your lovingkindness in the morning, for in You do I trust; Cause me to know the way in which I should walk, for I lift my soul to You."
Psalm 143:8

LIFE IS FULL OF DISAPPOINTMENTS.
BUT INSTEAD OF BEING DEFINED BY THEM, I WILL REMEMBER
THAT I AM THE CHILD OF A GOD WHO LOVES ME.

"Can a woman forget her nursing child, And not have compassion on the son of her womb?
Surely they may forget, Yet I will not forget you."
Isaiah 49:15

YOUR EYES ARE UNFLINCHING
AS YOU GAZE DEEPLY INTO MY SOUL
YOUR SEARCH LEAVES NOTHING HIDDEN
AND ALL MY NEEDS I TRUST YOU KNOW

"O Lord, You have searched me and known me.
You know my sitting down and my rising up; You understand my thought afar off."
Psalm 139:1-2

IN THE MOURNING WHEN I RISE
GIVE ME JESUS

IN THE MOURNING WHEN I RISE
HELP ME JESUS

IN THE MOURNING WHEN I RISE
HOLD ME JESUS

IN THE MORNING WHEN I RISE
THANK YOU JESUS

"It is good to give thanks to the Lord, And to sing praises to Your name, O Most High; To declare Your lovingkindness in the morning, And Your faithfulness every night," Psalm 92:1-2

I CAN HAVE A POSITIVE OUTLOOK IN
THE MIDST OF EVERYTHING GOING
ON AROUND ME BECAUSE I KEEP
MY EYES ON YOU

"A merry heart
does good, like
medicine…"
Proverbs 17:22

HANGING PRECARIOUSLY FROM YOUR
AERIAL TRAPEZE,
YOU SWING TO AND FRO BY GENTLE BREEZE,
THEN TO OUR DISMAY YOU LET GO

YET WITH ARTFUL POISE AND GYMNASTIC FLAIR,
YOU TWIST AND TUMBLE THROUGH THE AIR THEN
WITH CHOREOGRAPHED SKILL AND GRACE
YOU STICK YOUR LANDING AND WIN YOUR PLACE

AND AT THAT MOMENT WE APPLAUD
THE MASTERFUL WORK OF THE
CREATOR GOD

"Many, O Lord my God, are Your wonderful works which You have done; And Your thoughts toward us cannot be recounted to You in order; If I would declare and speak of them, they are more than can be numbered."
Psalm 40:5

MAY THE
OUTPOURING OF
GOD'S LOVE
FLOW FREELY INTO
THE RECESSES OF
YOUR SOUL

"For I have
satiated the
weary soul, and I
have replenished
every sorrowful
soul."
Jeremiah 31:25

YOU FOUND ME,
THEN SHOWED ME THAT EVEN
IN MY BROKENNESS I STILL HAVE VALUE

"My flesh and
my heart fail;
But God is the
strength of my
heart and my
portion forever."
Psalm 73:26

FRIENDS MAY:
LOOK DIFFERENT FROM US
ACT DIFFERENT FROM US
THINK DIFFERENT FROM US

BUT THERE IS ALWAYS ONE
THING WE HAVE IN COMMON:

TRUE FRIENDS ARE A
GIFT FROM GOD

"A man who has
friends must
himself be
friendly, but there
is a friend who
sticks closer than
a brother."
Proverbs 18:24

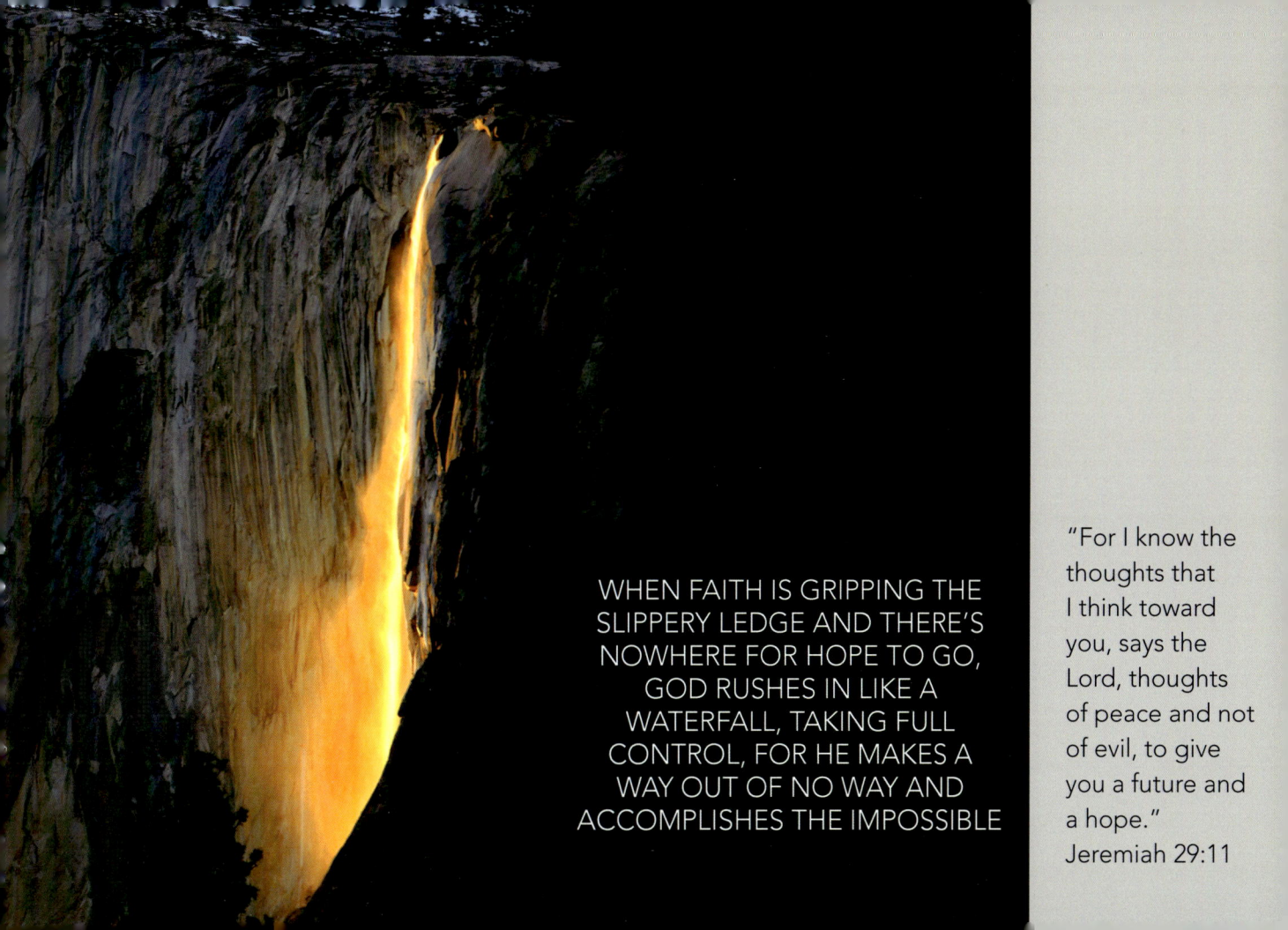

WHEN FAITH IS GRIPPING THE
SLIPPERY LEDGE AND THERE'S
NOWHERE FOR HOPE TO GO,
GOD RUSHES IN LIKE A
WATERFALL, TAKING FULL
CONTROL, FOR HE MAKES A
WAY OUT OF NO WAY AND
ACCOMPLISHES THE IMPOSSIBLE

"For I know the
thoughts that
I think toward
you, says the
Lord, thoughts
of peace and not
of evil, to give
you a future and
a hope."
Jeremiah 29:11

"For I will be merciful to their unrighteousness, and their sins and their lawless deeds I will remember no more."
Hebrews 8:12

EVERY MEMORY THAT CAUSES MY HEART TO ACHE
AND GUILT THAT KEEPS ME WIDE AWAKE,
GOD FORMS A MIST AND CARRIES TO SEA
THAT ANGUISH DEEP INSIDE OF ME,
AND CASTS MY SINS TO A WATERY GRAVE
FOR WHAT I SURRENDERED, GOD FORGAVE

YOUR TENDER LOVE REFRESHES
MY SOUL AND ENABLES ME TO
SEE REFLECTIONS OF YOUR GRACE

"You, O God,
sent a plentiful
rain, whereby
You confirmed
Your inheritance,
when it was
weary."
Psalm 68:9

THE EVENING SUN STRETCHES ITS WARM BLANKET
OVER MY EXHAUSTION WHILE MY FATHER LEANS OVER
HEAVEN AND GENTLY WHISPERS TO MY SOUL TO EXHALE;
AND WITH HEAVY EYES I PEACEFULLY SURRENDER

"I will both lie down in peace, and sleep; for You alone, O Lord, make me dwell in safety."
Psalm 4:8

MY PRAYERS ARE FROZEN, HELD IN
TIME, YOU DO NOT HEAR MY CRY,
EACH WORD I UTTER SEEMS TO
FREEZE ON GLACIERS, MILES HIGH,

YET GLACIERS ARE ALWAYS MOVING,
CHANGING THE WORLD IN WAYS I
CANNOT SEE,
AND PRAYER ALSO HAS THE POWER
TO CHANGE LIVES, AND MOST OF ALL,
CHANGE ME

NOW I APPROACH YOU THANKFUL THAT I
CAN COME BOLDLY TO YOUR THRONE
AND FIND ANSWERS TO MY PRAYERS IN
WAYS I'VE NEVER THOUGHT OR KNOWN

"Hear my cry,
O God; Attend
to my prayer.
From the end
of the earth I
will cry to You,
When my heart
is overwhelmed;
Lead me to
the rock that is
higher than I."
Psalm 61:1-2

"Peace I leave with you, My peace I give to you; not as the world gives do I give to you. Let not your heart be troubled, neither let it be afraid."
John 14:27

AT THE CLOSE OF EACH DAY
I AM REMINDED THAT YOU ARE THE ONE WHO AWAKENS ME,
THE ONE WHO GETS ME THROUGH THE DAY, AND THE
ONE WHO CONTINUALLY KEEPS ME IN YOUR CARE